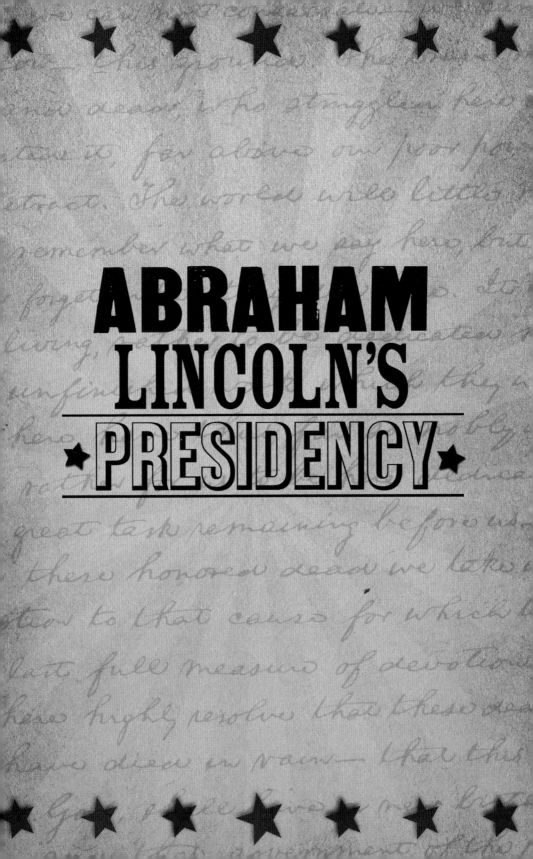

ABRAHAM
LINCOLN'S
★ PRESIDENCY ★

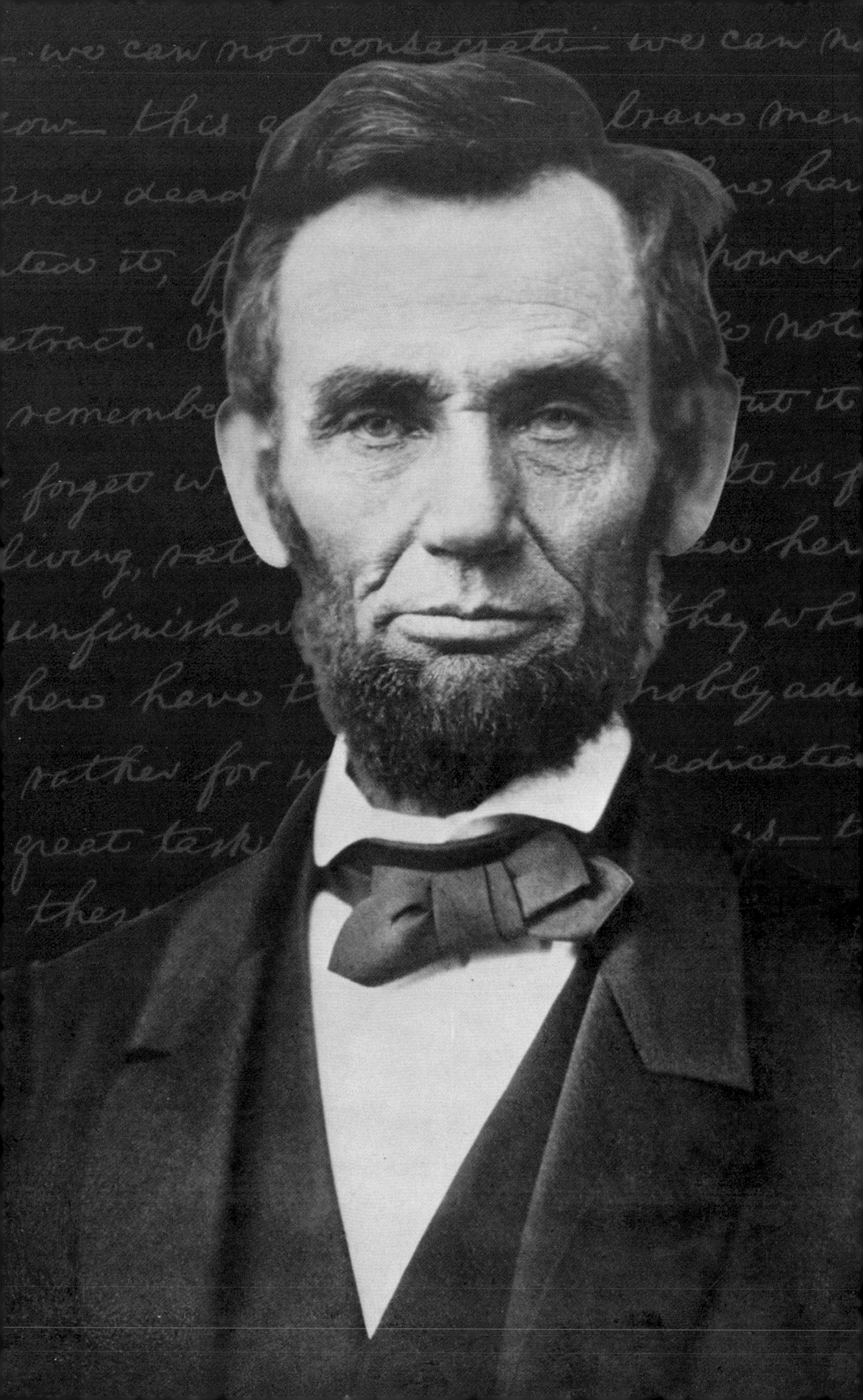
we can not consecrate— we can
this brave men
retract.
remember
living,
unfinished
here have to
rather for
great task
these

$\mathcal{P}$RESIDENTIAL $\mathcal{P}$OWERHOUSES

ABRAHAM LINCOLN'S
★ PRESIDENCY ★

KAREN LATCHANA KENNEY
CATHERINE M. ANDRONIK

LERNER PUBLICATIONS ◆ MINNEAPOLIS

Lerner Publications Company
A division of Lerner Publishing Group, Inc.
241 First Avenue North
Minneapolis, MN 55401 USA

For reading levels and more information, look up this title at www.lernerbooks.com.

Main body text set in Caecilia LT Std 9.5/15.
Typeface provided by Adobe Systems.

Library of Congress Cataloging-in-Publication Data

Names: Kenney, Karen Latchana. | Andronik, Catherine M.
Title: Abraham Lincoln's presidency / by Karen Latchana Kenney and Catherine M. Andronik.
Description: Minneapolis, MN : Lerner Publications, [2016] | Series: Presidential powerhouses | Includes bibliographical references and index.
Identifiers: LCCN 2015013552| ISBN 9781467779258 (lb : alk. paper) | ISBN 9781467785471 (eb pdf)
Subjects: LCSH: Lincoln, Abraham, 1809–1865—Juvenile literature. | Presidents—United States—Biography—Juvenile literature. | United States—Politics and government—1861–1865—Juvenile literature.
Classification: LCC E457.905 .K36 2016 | DDC 973.7092—dc23

LC record available at http://lccn.loc.gov/2015013552

Manufactured in the United States of America
1 – VP – 7/15/16

★ TABLE OF CONTENTS ★

★ INTRODUCTION ★

A crowd gathered in a field outside the small town of Gettysburg, Pennsylvania, on a chilly afternoon in November 1863. Four months earlier, Gettysburg had seen one of the fiercest battles of the American Civil War (1861–1865). Two years before that, the country had split into the proslavery South and the antislavery North. The nation was now at war.

On July 1, 1863, General Robert E. Lee had led the Confederate forces of the South to Gettysburg to confront Union forces in the North. After three days, Union soldiers, under General George Meade, drove Lee's troops back. About 50,000 soldiers from both sides were casualties—killed, wounded, captured, or missing. An estimated 3,155 Union soldiers and 4,708 Confederate soldiers lay dead.

The dead bodies would decay quickly in the summer heat, so the soldiers were hastily buried in graves in the surrounding countryside. Pennsylvania's governor set aside land for an official cemetery at Gettysburg where the Union soldiers could be reburied with honor and ceremony. After the war, most of the Confederate dead were reburied in the South.

Crowds gathered for the cemetery's dedication on November 19. Famous speechmaker Edward Everett was to be the main speaker, and an additional guest was invited to share his thoughts: President Abraham Lincoln.

Everett spoke first. A gifted orator, he used beautiful turns of phrase at Gettysburg to speak for two hours about poetry and history. The crowd listened in silence, some people moved to tears.

In 1863 the United States was in the midst of a bitter civil war. Dead soldiers cover this battlefield at Gettysburg, Pennsylvania, in July.

LINCOLN'S SPEECH

Then Lincoln stepped up to the podium. He had carefully crafted his speech, writing and rewriting it over several days. In contrast to Everett, Lincoln spoke for only two minutes. His words were heartfelt, for he had visited many battlefields, met many soldiers, and seen death and destruction in his own life. The struggles tearing apart the nation hurt him deeply. He appealed to the crowd's patriotism and provided reassurance that the prolonged conflict was serving a meaningful cause worth suffering for. Delivering what is known as the Gettysburg Address, Lincoln began by reminding the crowd that their ancestors had created a new country only "fourscore and seven years ago," or eighty-seven years ago. Lincoln was referring to 1776, when the founders of the United States had signed the Declaration of Independence.

Among other things, the document offered a promise that in the new nation, "all men are created equal." Now, Lincoln said, Americans were fighting to see if a nation based on the ideals of liberty and equality could survive.

He told the audience,

> [The] brave men, living and dead, who struggled here, have consecrated it, far above our poor power to add or detract. The world will little note, nor long remember what we say here, but it can never forget what [these soldiers] did here. . . . It is rather for us to be here dedicated to the great task remaining before us . . . that we here highly resolve that these dead shall not have died in vain—that this nation, under God, shall have a new birth of freedom—and that government of the people, by the people, for the people, shall not perish from the earth.

Lincoln's speech, which was printed in newspapers around the country, solidified Union support for the war and renewed hope that the nation could come together again and heal its wounds. Everett sent a letter of praise to Lincoln, saying, "I should be glad if I could flatter myself that I came as near to the central idea of the occasion in two hours as you did in two minutes."

THE WORLD TAKES NOTE

Lincoln said at Gettysburg that the world wouldn't note his words. He was wrong. In a eulogy for Lincoln after the president's death in 1865, Senator Charles Sumner recalled the president's speech. "The world noted at once what he said, and will never cease to remember it," the senator said. "The battle itself was less important than the speech." More than 150 years later, Lincoln's speech remains one of the most famous examples of American oratory, and schoolchildren still study it.

President Abraham Lincoln delivers his Gettysburg Address on November 19, 1863.

The man who spoke the powerful words at Gettysburg had been president for two and a half years. Lincoln had risen from a poor background to become the leader of the country during one of its most trying times. He would live for only a year and a half after the speech. An assassin's bullet cut his life short on April 14,1865, just five days after the South surrendered and only shortly after Lincoln had begun his second term as president.

First sworn in as president in 1861, Lincoln would steer the country in a new direction—toward the "new birth of freedom" for *all* Americans, as he had spoken of at Gettysburg. Fighting to hold the country together, he used presidential powers as no president had before. Future wartime presidents would look to the examples he set. His policies would help connect Americans and lead to unprecedented growth of the United States. Under his leadership, as Lincoln had said at Gettysburg, democracy would not "perish from the earth."

★ CHAPTER ONE ★

FROM HUMBLE ORIGINS

The small town of Hodgenville, Kentucky, was part of the American western frontier in the early nineteenth century. Thomas and Nancy Lincoln and their young daughter, Sarah, lived nearby on a small farm. Their home was a one-room log cabin with a dirt floor that Thomas had built. There on February 12, 1809, Abraham Lincoln was born.

Abraham's parents were about the same age as the United States in 1783, which had won its independence from Great Britain only twenty-six years earlier. Thomas was a hardworking farmer and carpenter. Like many people on the frontier, Thomas was illiterate, but he was also a gifted storyteller, as Abraham would be too.

Thomas Lincoln, Abraham's father, opposed slavery.

Thomas Lincoln built the family's log cabin in Hodgenville, Kentucky (like this reproduction above). Abraham was born there on February 12, 1809.

Nancy and Thomas opposed slavery, which was legal in Kentucky at the time. They attended a Baptist church where they heard antislavery sermons. When Abraham was three, a second son was born. He lived only a few days.

In 1816 the family moved west into Indiana. Abraham helped his father clear, plow, and harvest farm fields; cut down trees; and split logs into rails for fences. He also took care of the farm animals, but hunting and shooting animals disgusted him.

Two years after they arrived, tragedy struck the Lincoln family and their community. The milk of some local cows became deadly after the animals ate the poisonous plant white snakeroot. People who drank the milk became ill with a disease called milk sickness. Thirty-four-year-old Nancy Lincoln was one of several who died. Her nine-year-old son, Abraham, helped his father build her coffin.

FRONTIER LIFE

The year after his mother's death was bitterly sad for Abraham. His sister, Sarah, took care of him and did the household chores. A year later, his father remarried. His new wife was a loving woman: Sarah "Sally" Bush Johnston Lincoln. Sally was a widow with three children. With books among her possessions—a rare luxury then—she brought some sophistication to the frontier cabin. She became a kind and good mother to Abraham and his sister, and the boy always called his stepmother Mama.

With few schools and teachers on the frontier, education was hard to come by. Farming and chores took up nearly every day of every season. Altogether, Abraham attended one year of school, off and on between the ages of eleven and fifteen. His education was uninspiring, but "Somehow I could read, write, and [solve basic math problems]," Lincoln later said. Learning to read opened

Sarah "Sally" Bush Johnston married Thomas Lincoln on December 2, 1819. She was a kind stepmother to Abraham.

Farmwork and chores kept Abraham from attending school for a formal education. He taught himself mostly by reading books.

up a world of self-education for Abraham. An avid reader, he was deeply curious and developed his natural skill for language, and he loved to tell stories and jokes.

Sally encouraged Abraham in his love of learning, though his father was not supportive. Later, Abraham would say that no son could love a mother more than he loved Sally. When Abraham was seventeen, he lost another person he loved when his sister, Sarah, died during pregnancy.

ENTERING POLITICS

In 1830 the Lincolns moved from Indiana to Illinois, enticed by reports of good soil. Illinois residents had voted to outlaw slavery eight years earlier. Some people objected to slavery on the grounds that it was morally wrong to enslave other human beings. Others objected that slavery created unfair competition for work. Slaveholders received the benefit of unpaid slave labor, for example, while free laborers had to be self-sufficient.

Abraham decided to leave the farm and pursue politics and the law instead of farming.

By this time, Abraham had grown tall—6 feet 4 inches (1.9 meters)—and strong. He was ambitious, intelligent, and knew he could be more than a poor farmer. When he was twenty-one, Lincoln left home to live in New Salem, outside Springfield, Illinois. There, he ran a general store, and later borrowed money to buy his own store.

The community welcomed this friendly newcomer and his funny stories. He won a reputation for being honest and helpful, and he continued educating himself by borrowing books on a wide range of subjects and going to political meetings.

Just twenty-three years old, Lincoln ran in 1832 for his first political position, to serve in the state legislature. He presented himself as a common workingman, with humor and good sense. "If elected I will be thankful," he said in a speech. "If beaten, I can do as I have been doing, work for a living."

The young politician was in favor of large-scale projects to improve the state's infrastructure, such as building bridges and railroads. He also supported a national banking system because the United States did not yet have a standard form of paper money. Individual banks printed their own currency and negotiated loans on their own terms. Settlers such as

Thomas Lincoln had lived and worked without banks. They often bartered, trading their work for goods instead of money. But Lincoln knew that big, expensive projects needed a standardized financial system.

Soon after his decision to run for office, the Black Hawk War (May–August 1832) broke out. Lincoln joined the Illinois militia, a group of volunteer soldiers. He planned to be back in time for the August elections. To his surprise, his company of militiamen elected him their captain, which he later said was "a success which gave me more pleasure than any I have had since." He served for three months, and though he never fought, his service boosted his self-confidence.

Members of the Sauk and Fox American Indian nations flee from the Battle of Bad Axe during the Black Hawk War in 1832.

THE BLACK HAWK WAR

A federal treaty in 1804 forced the American Indian Sauk and Fox people to leave their homelands in Illinois and move west of the Mississippi River to Iowa. Under the leadership of Black Hawk, a Sauk warrior, more than one thousand American Indians returned to reclaim their lands in Illinois in April 1832. Their arrival incited fear among the white population, which responded with a force of seven thousand men, including state and federal militias as well as some American Indians who opposed Black Hawk.

Over the summer months, a series of battles led to a bloody attack at Bad Axe River in Wisconsin, where US soldiers massacred American Indian men, women, and children. By August an estimated 450 to 600 American Indians and 70 whites had been killed. Black Hawk surrendered, and by 1837, American Indians had been forced to move farther west.

Black Hawk led more than a thousand American Indians in a campaign to return to their homeland.

When Lincoln returned to New Salem, he lost the election, but his popularity won him 277 out of the 300 votes in his town. He continued to work hard. His store had failed, and he owed a lot of money to creditors. Instead of declaring bankruptcy, he cut rails of wood; delivered mail for the post office; and worked as a surveyor, measuring land. His experiences shaped his belief in the importance of self-sufficiency and the power of work to improve one's place in life.

Lincoln ran for the state legislature again in 1834, and this time, he won. He served four two-year terms, establishing laws for Illinois.

Lincoln was a member of the Whig Party, a new political party in favor of modernization and of a strong federal government. As Lincoln later said, the government should "do for the people what needs to be done, but which they can not, by individual effort, do at all, or do so well, for themselves." Whigs like Lincoln supported government-funded improvement projects, such as building roads and better communication systems. The printing press was the main form of mass communication in this era, and it could take weeks to send a newspaper or a letter across the country. In 1832 Samuel Morse began developing the telegraph to send electrical signals over wires. The technology rapidly sped up communication.

After becoming a legislator, Lincoln began studying to become a lawyer. At the time, lawyers didn't need a college degree, and Lincoln taught himself from law books he borrowed. Lincoln received his license to practice law on September 9, 1836.

As he studied the law, Lincoln was also forming his political views on slavery. He saw it as a disease that hurt the democratic ideals of the country. Hardworking himself, Lincoln believed

VOTING RIGHTS

During Abraham Lincoln's life, voting rights varied from state to state. Generally speaking, only white male citizens could vote in every state. Women and people of color could not. Some states required that residents own property or be US-born to vote. Lincoln wrote a letter to a newspaper on June 13, 1836, supporting voting rights for all white people, men and women alike. Everyone who shared the burden of government, he wrote, should share the privileges too. "Consequently I go for admitting all whites to the right of suffrage [voting], who pay taxes or bear arms, (by no means excluding females.)" A dozen years later, in 1848, members of the first women's rights convention would meet in Seneca Falls, New York, calling for women's right to vote. Lincoln, however, never spoke up again for women's suffrage.

that slave labor took away from the dignity of work. All workers deserved payment for their labors, and it was unfair and selfish for someone such as a slave owner to take what they hadn't earned. He thought everyone should be able to better themselves by their own work, the way he had.

Yet in Lincoln's opinion, the government could not legally abolish, or officially end, slavery overnight. It was too ingrained in the South's politics and economy. Furthermore, the US Constitution acknowledged slavery. The founders of the Constitution had allowed slaveholding states to count each slave as three-fifths of a person for purposes of taxation and representation in the federal government.

Lincoln greatly respected the Constitution, and in his view, Congress had no constitutional authority to ban slavery in the South. Only a constitutional amendment could outlaw slavery. This was unlikely since congressional representatives from the South would not support such a change. Lincoln felt strongly that the government should not allow slavery to spread. He and other antislavery Americans hoped that if slavery were contained, it would die out. He decided to vote against proslavery legislation, and on March 3, 1837, he made his first official protest against slavery before the legislature.

This illustration depicts a group of slaves chained together in the early nineteenth century.

This 1837 photograph of Lincoln was taken during his time as a lawyer and a state legislator in Springfield, Illinois.

Soon fellow Illinois legislator John Todd Stuart invited Lincoln to join his law practice in the new state capital of Springfield, Illinois. Lincoln accepted and moved to Springfield in April 1837. There he began a busy law career that earned him a good living. At thirty years old, he had not yet married but would soon meet his future wife.

MARY TODD

Twenty-one-year-old Mary Todd came from one of Kentucky's wealthiest families. Her father, Robert Todd, was a successful businessman who was well-connected in the Whig Party to which Lincoln belonged. Her father was also a slave owner.

Mary Todd did not support slavery. She had an excellent education for a woman of her era, having attended a boarding

school where she learned French, social skills, and dancing. She could hold political conversations from a young age. Todd thought that Lincoln had a promising future, despite his lack of social graces, and they had a lot in common. They had both lost a mother at a young age, and they both were politically ambitious.

In the late 1830s, Todd was living in Springfield with her sister Elizabeth and Elizabeth's husband, wealthy businessman Ninian Edwards. The couple regularly hosted the social elite at their home. Lincoln and Todd first met at a dance there in December 1839. Todd later remembered the moment well. "Miss Todd," Lincoln said as he approached her, "I want to dance with you in the worst way."

By the next summer, Todd and Lincoln were courting. Elizabeth and Ninian Edwards, however, rejected Lincoln for his rough background. They believed he did not have a secure future.

Although Mary Todd came from a wealthy family in Kentucky, she and Lincoln had similar values and ambitions.

LINCOLN'S DEPRESSION

Lincoln was well known among his friends for having a melancholy nature, despite being an avid joke teller. After breaking up with Mary Todd, Lincoln's depression worsened, and a doctor diagnosed him as having what was then called hypochondria, or hypo. At the time, doctors believed hypo was a form of depression a little less severe than madness.

Lincoln missed a week in the legislature during treatments for his hypo. Doctors misunderstood depression, and their harsh treatments included bloodletting, vomiting and diarrhea induced by mercury (a poisonous metal that is now known to increase

moodiness), and fasting, followed by large doses of black pepper or ginger. Lincoln's treatment left him emaciated and weary. Lincoln would continue to suffer bouts of depression throughout his life. He wrestled with his moods and drove himself to pursue meaningful work despite his depression.

Lincoln suffered from depression during his life.

The rejection devastated Lincoln, who fell into a deep depression and broke off the engagement for a time in 1841. He went to stay with a friend in slaveholding Kentucky. On the way home, he saw a line of twelve enslaved men chained together. The sight of human bondage, he later said, "was a continual torment to me."

Lincoln and Todd eventually reconnected and became engaged. They married in November 1842.

★ CHAPTER TWO ★

TO WASHINGTON, DC, AND BACK AGAIN

braham and Mary Lincoln's first son, Robert Todd Lincoln, was born in 1843. The following year, the family welcomed Edward (Eddie) Baker Lincoln. Lincoln was a fond and easygoing father.

When his first two sons were toddlers, Lincoln was elected to represent Illinois in the US House of Representatives in 1846. The family moved by stagecoach, steamboat, and train to the nation's capital, Washington, DC.

A NEW CONGRESSMAN

Early in Lincoln's term, the Mexican-American War (1846–1848) broke out over the question of Texas's boundaries and where the United States ended. Mexico had originally controlled the region, but Texas had fought for and won independence from Mexico in 1836. The United States took control of Texas from Mexico in March 1845. The slaveholding South had approved this plan to annex Texas, since in this new state, slavery would be legal. In April 1846, a skirmish between Mexican and US forces along the disputed US-Mexico border left more than a dozen US soldiers dead. Claiming an invasion, Congress declared war on Mexico in May.

Lincoln moved to Washington, DC, to represent Illinois at the Capitol (above, with its unfinished dome) in 1846.

Lincoln agreed with his fellow Whigs who had not supported annexing Texas, fearing the expansion of slavery, and Lincoln spoke out against the war. His voice was ignored. In 1848 Mexico lost the war and ceded to the United States land that became the states of New Mexico, Utah, Nevada, Arizona, California, Texas, and western Colorado for $15 million.

Lincoln's opposition to the Mexican-American War was seen as unpatriotic, and Illinois voters did not reelect him. When his two-year term ended, Lincoln worried his political life was over.

He practiced law in Springfield again, becoming a top lawyer in his state and earning a reputation as tough and convincing in the courtroom. Among other things, Lincoln specialized in cases about patents for newly invented steam-powered farm machinery. Inventions such as mechanical reapers to harvest crops could do the work of many hands. Lincoln hoped this new technology would help end the South's dependence on slave labor.

Disputes over the border between Texas and Mexico eventually led to the Mexican-American War. In this painting, US forces fire upon Mexican forces during the Battle of Veracruz in March 1847.

Lincoln's career flourished, but his family life was sometimes rocky. Mary Lincoln was moody, and Lincoln spent a lot of time in his law office. They were both devastated when their second son, Eddie, died of a lung disease in 1850, shortly before his fourth birthday. Their third child, William (Willie) Wallace Lincoln, was born on December 21, 1850. Thomas Lincoln, Abraham's father, died the next month. Lincoln had never been close to his father and did not go to his funeral.

In 1853 the Lincolns' last child was born. Thomas, a lively boy nicknamed Tad (for tadpole), would become his father's favorite.

ISSUE OF SLAVERY

Slavery increasingly became a major issue of national debate as the United States expanded westward and more and more states

joined the Union. New states generally started out first as territories under federal rule. When their population was big enough, they could petition the government for full statehood. Citizens hotly debated whether slavery should be allowed in new territories. And who should decide: the federal government or politicians and voters in each new territory or state?

SLAVERY AND COTTON IN THE SOUTH

A Dutch ship brought the first enslaved Africans to the American colonies in 1619. In the 1780s, when the framers of the US Constitution agreed to allow slavery to continue in the new nation, many thought it would soon die out on its own. By the time of the American Civil War, however, US slave owners held about four million people as slaves. In fact, one of every three people in the South was a slave.

The growth of slavery was driven mainly by the cotton industry. In 1794 Eli Whitney patented his invention of the cotton gin. This machine made it easier to process cotton quickly, and cotton soon became one of the biggest-selling and most lucrative crops in the United States. By 1850 the South was producing 2.5 million bales of cotton each year. It supplied most of the raw cotton that textile factories in the North and in Great Britain and other European countries relied upon. Southern cotton plantations relied on forced labor to produce the crop, and as the cotton industry grew, it demanded more and more slaves to produce higher volumes of cotton.

Stephen Douglas argued that settlers in a new territory should decide whether slavery was legal in that region.

The question was dividing the country. In 1820 a law called the Missouri Compromise had tried to strike a balance by outlawing slavery in any new states north of the Mason-Dixon Line, a geographical division between traditional slaveholding states and free states. In 1854 the Kansas-Nebraska Act opened these two regions for new settlement. Both Kansas and Nebraska were north of the demarcation line, and the act allowed voters in the new territories to decide the question of slavery for themselves. It reversed the limits to slavery that the Missouri Compromise had set.

The main sponsor of the Kansas-Nebraska Act of 1854 was Stephen Douglas, a senator from Illinois. Douglas supported the idea of popular sovereignty, or popular rule—the right of settlers, not the federal government, to choose whether to permit slavery in a new state or territory. Since only white men could vote, this meant that they alone would decide whether it was legal to enslave African American men, women, and children.

Lincoln stated that the Kansas-Nebraska Act was a "great moral wrong and injustice." He derided Douglas's idea of popular sovereignty. In a speech in 1854, he said that the country "began by declaring all men are equal" and had been reduced to declaring that "for *some* men to enslave *others* is a 'sacred right of self-government.'"

The issue of slavery in the territories became violent. Southern proslavery groups clashed many times with antislavery groups from the North in what became known as Bloody Kansas. Violence even broke out in Congress when Representative Preston Brooks of South Carolina beat Senator Charles Sumner of Massachusetts almost to death on the Senate floor. Brooks was angry because Sumner had delivered an antislavery speech in which he insulted a proslavery senator who was related to Brooks.

Violence over the issue of slavery was spreading across the country and dividing Congress. Representative Preston Brooks (left) badly beat Senator Charles Sumner on the Senate floor for his antislavery views.

A HOUSE DIVIDED

In 1858 Lincoln ran for the US Senate to represent Illinois in Washington, DC. The Whigs were falling apart as a party over the issue of slavery, so Lincoln left the Whigs to join the new antislavery Republican Party.

The Republicans gathered for their convention in June in Springfield to choose their senatorial candidate. Anticipating that he would win the nomination, Lincoln wrote an acceptance speech. He mostly addressed the issue of slavery, saying it was tearing the country apart and calling for settling the question one way or another. Several of his colleagues thought the speech would be viewed as too extreme, but Mary Lincoln advised her husband to keep it as it was. She told him, "It will make you president."

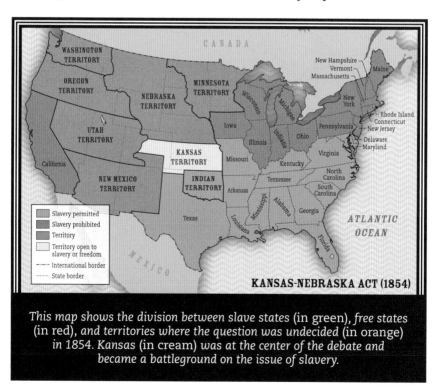

KANSAS-NEBRASKA ACT (1854)

This map shows the division between slave states (in green), free states (in red), and territories where the question was undecided (in orange) in 1854. Kansas (in cream) was at the center of the debate and became a battleground on the issue of slavery.

Lincoln delivered the speech on June 16, 1858, upon accepting his party's nomination. Comparing the United States to a house, he quoted from the Bible, "A house divided against itself cannot stand." Lincoln continued,

> I believe this government cannot endure, permanently half-slave and half free. I do not expect the Union to be dissolved—I do not expect the house to fall—but I do expect it will cease to be divided. It will become all one thing, or all the other.

Newspapers around the country printed the "House Divided" speech, which spread Lincoln's fame far and wide. To proslavery ears, his sentiments sounded like threats. The country could continue as it was, Stephen Douglas contended. He warned that Lincoln's ideas would lead the country into war.

THE RISE OF NEWSPAPERS

The nineteenth century saw the rapid rise of newspapers in the United States. In 1800 the nation had two hundred newspapers, and by 1860, it had three thousand. New printing technology allowed for newspapers to be printed quickly and efficiently. Demand for the news was driven by a growing middle class who took an interest in politics, by higher literacy rates, and by more leisure time for reading. Newspapers blatantly supported one political party over all others, spinning fabricated stories to support their views. The so-called facts depended on which newspaper a person read.

THE LINCOLN-DOUGLAS DEBATES

Douglas was the incumbent Lincoln had to beat to become senator. Nicknamed the Little Giant, Douglas stood only 5 feet 4 inches (1.6 m), but he was a powerful force in politics and, like Lincoln, a skilled orator.

Lincoln challenged Douglas to debate him. Douglas accepted and proposed seven debates to be held across Illinois. The two politicians were worthy adversaries. Immediately and overwhelmingly, the main issue in each debate was slavery.

Douglas played to the prejudices and fears of the time. He called Republicans who advocated the abolition of slavery Black Republicans. If slavery ended, he warned, African Americans would come to Illinois to take white men's jobs, even though the state's constitution barred this. He pushed for popular sovereignty, allowing each new state or territory to decide the issue for itself. He called Lincoln a radical and denounced Lincoln's position that slavery was morally wrong. Douglas said, "I believe this government . . . was made by white men, for the benefit of white men and their posterity forever."

Lincoln (standing at center) and Douglas (seated at left) participated in a series of debates during the 1858 campaign for a seat in the US Senate.

Lincoln repeated his creed that all men are created equal and that the government should not allow slavery to spread. He did have some racial prejudices, and he assured listeners, especially in southern Illinois, that he didn't think African American and white people were social equals. On the issue of work, however, Lincoln had no doubts. "In the right to eat the bread of his labor without the [permission] of anyone else," he said, "the slave is my equal and the equal of . . . every living man."

Lincoln also disagreed with Douglas about the US Supreme Court's 1857 decision in the *Dred Scott v. Sanford* case. The court's ruling had stated that slaves were not citizens and therefore were not protected under the Constitution. It also called into question the federal government's legal right to keep slavery out of new territories. Douglas felt the ruling was a victory, while Lincoln did not.

Slaves pick cotton on a plantation in Savannah, Georgia, circa 1860s.

THE DRED SCOTT DECISION

Dred and Harriet Scott were a married couple who were enslaved by John Emerson, a US Army doctor. Like most military personnel, Emerson was posted in various places around the United States, sometimes in states that permitted slavery, such as Louisiana or Missouri, and sometimes in states that did not permit slavery, such as the Wisconsin Territory and Illinois. The doctor brought the Scott family along to his various postings.

When Emerson died, Dred Scott tried to buy freedom from Emerson's widow, Irene, for himself, his wife, and their children. Irene Emerson refused. Scott sued her, stating that he had been wrongly held in bondage in states where slavery was illegal. At first, in a Missouri court, Scott won his plea, but the decision was later overturned. In 1857 the case went all the way to the US Supreme Court. The highest court in the land ruled against Scott. It stated that the framers of the Constitution did not mean to include African American people in their democracy. No African Americans—slave or free— were citizens, and they could not file a lawsuit. Slaveholders supported the ruling, while opponents of slavery, such as Lincoln, did not.

Dred Scott went to court to fight for his and his family's freedom in 1857.

Journalists followed the debates closely, publishing the speeches along with biased stories on the two politicians. Until 1858 Lincoln had not been well known outside Springfield and Washington, DC. Thanks to the newspaper coverage, Lincoln gained wider recognition.

On November 2, 1858, Douglas won the Senate race by a vote of 54–46. Lincoln was disappointed, but another, more important, election loomed just two years in the future—the 1860 race for the presidency.

★ CHAPTER THREE ★

WINNING THE PRESIDENCY

As political parties prepared for the 1860 presidential election, the United States was more divided on the question of slavery than it had ever been. Violence was on the rise.

AFRICAN AMERICAN REBELS AND THE RAID ON HARPERS FERRY

From the beginning, enslaved African Americans had found ways to rebel against slavery. Sometimes this took passive forms, such as breaking the master's tools. Violent revolts against slavery during the colonial era included the New York Slave Revolt of 1712 (slavery was not entirely outlawed in New York until 1827) and the 1739 Stono Rebellion in South Carolina. Starting in the early nineteenth century, black and white organizers of the secret Underground Railroad—a network of escape routes and abolitionists—helped many thousands of enslaved people escape to free states or Canada.

In 1831 slave rebel Nat Turner led a group of more than fifty free and enslaved African Americans from plantation to plantation in Virginia, killing dozens of white people. Nat Turner's Rebellion

terrified white people in the South, who clamped down on the rights of black people afterward. Legislators passed laws restricting African Americans' access to education, ownership of livestock, and their freedom to preach or to meet in groups.

In October 1859, radical abolitionist John Brown led about twenty men in a raid on a federal weapons arsenal in the town of Harpers Ferry, Virginia. Brown and sixteen of the other abolitionists were white, and the others were African Americans. Brown tried but failed to recruit more African American rebels to the group, whose mission was to spark a widespread slave uprising. After two days of fighting, Brown and most of the rebels were killed or captured by US Marines led by Colonel Robert E. Lee.

A court sentenced Brown to die by hanging. On the morning of his execution, he wrote that slavery would never end peacefully

US Marines break into the armory at Harpers Ferry to capture abolitionist John Brown and his raiders in October 1859.

but could be purged only by blood. News of the raid quickly spread in the South. Some Democratic newspapers incorrectly linked people in the North—most of whom were Republicans who did not support slavery—with support of Brown's actions. Stephen Douglas even stated that the Harpers Ferry incident was the natural result of Republican teachings. Many in the South were sure that a Republican president would mean the end of slavery and life as they knew it.

CHOOSING CANDIDATES

In this time of upheaval, President James Buchanan, a Democrat, chose not to run for reelection. Both the Democrats and Republicans would therefore be choosing new candidates for the presidential election of 1860.

The proslavery South threatened to secede, or leave the Union, if an antislavery Republican won the election. As the parties began choosing candidates, it seemed likely that the next president would be a Republican. The proslavery Democratic Party could not find common ground among its members and broke into splinter groups, each with its own candidate. This weakened the party and split its supporters.

On April 23, 1860, the Democrats convened in Charleston, South Carolina, to choose a candidate. The favorite was Stephen Douglas, who had defeated Lincoln for the Senate seat in 1858. The more extreme proslavery Democrats, nicknamed Fire-Eaters, however, wanted a candidate who would insist on stronger protections for slave owners and a clear statement that slavery would be legal in the growing West. They threatened to secede if they did not get their way. When fifty Fire-Eater delegates from the South stormed out of the convention, the meeting broke up. By June the Democrats in the north had nominated Douglas as the party's candidate for president. The Fire-Eaters and their

The Democratic Party met in Charleston, South Carolina, in April 1860 to choose a presidential candidate. The convention ended in a deadlock when members couldn't agree on a candidate.

supporters separately nominated then vice president John Breckinridge of Kentucky, a Democrat who supported slavery.

Meanwhile, the Republican Party met in May in Chicago, Illinois, to choose its candidate, and on May 18, delegates settled on Lincoln. In Lincoln's many speeches and writings, he had always said the government didn't have the legal power to abolish slavery where it already existed. Rather, he advocated limiting its spread into new territories. His views would appeal to Republican voters, and Lincoln's skills as a debater would make him an effective candidate.

CAMPAIGN AND ELECTION

Lincoln set up his campaign office in the Illinois Statehouse in Springfield. At that time, most candidates did not travel the country giving speeches during a campaign. Instead, hundreds of people came to visit Lincoln at the statehouse, bringing gifts and wanting to meet the new and relatively unknown candidate.

His supporters nicknamed him Rail Splitter, using his frontier background to appeal to working people. The name also represented Lincoln and his party's shared belief in free labor over slave labor.

News of the deep divisions within the Democratic Party gave Lincoln hope for a win. With so many proslavery candidates, it was unlikely that anyone would win a majority of votes in the South. He wrote to a friend, "It really appears now, as if the success of the Republican ticket is inevitable."

When Election Day arrived on November 6, 1860, Lincoln's name did not appear on ballots in ten states in the South, however. This was because no voter in those states would pledge to support him in the Electoral College. This group of representatives from each state casts votes for a president based on states' popular votes.

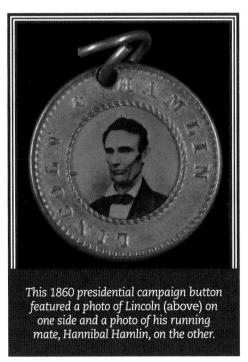

This 1860 presidential campaign button featured a photo of Lincoln (above) on one side and a photo of his running mate, Hannibal Hamlin, on the other.

At the time, a candidate's name could not appear on a state ballot without an electoral pledge, so Lincoln's name was absent from those ten states. As Lincoln had expected, no one Democratic candidate was able to win enough electoral votes to win the presidency. With 180 electoral votes, Lincoln had just enough to win. Lincoln received just less than 40 percent of the country's popular vote. The country could not have been more divided.

SMEARS AND THREATS

Southern reactions to Lincoln's candidacy were negative and even threatening. His effigy, or likeness, was burned in public. Southern papers attacked his looks and accused him of sending spies into the South to incite slave rebellions. Mobs beat up his suspected spies and arrested African Americans they thought supported Lincoln. Fire-Eaters told crowds that Lincoln would free the four million slaves and give them federal jobs in the South, a prospect that most listeners heard with horror. They also said African American men would marry white women, which especially horrified the many white supremacists who believed they were racially superior to black people.

Many white people in the South believed the propaganda, and these states threatened to secede if Lincoln were elected. Yet Lincoln did not believe the threats, stating, "The good people of the South have too much good sense and good temper to attempt the ruin of the government."

SECESSION BEGINS

The day after he was elected, Lincoln told reporters, "Well boys, your troubles are over now, mine have just begun." The president-elect could not have been more right. Just three weeks after his election, a secession movement was already gaining momentum in the South. Five states were planning to hold secession conventions. Voters in the South wanted to know, What was Lincoln's official policy on slavery? Could he assure the South that slavery would remain legal?

Lincoln had repeatedly stated that he would not abolish slavery where it already existed. He was firmly against slavery on principle and was committed to preventing its spread, which angered proslavery forces. Lincoln refused to make an official statement, fearing anything he said would be garbled by partisan newspapers to further inflame the South and ensure secession.

On December 20, 1860, the South Carolina secession convention met. The delegates unanimously voted to secede from the Union. Supporters of the move danced in the streets and set off cannons as they declared their freedom from what they feared was the threat of invasion and abolition from the North.

By February 4, 1861, six more states had seceded: Mississippi, Florida, Alabama, Georgia, Louisiana, and Texas. Representatives

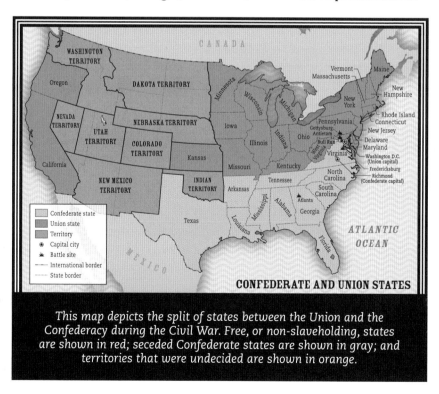

CONFEDERATE AND UNION STATES

This map depicts the split of states between the Union and the Confederacy during the Civil War. Free, or non-slaveholding, states are shown in red; seceded Confederate states are shown in gray; and territories that were undecided are shown in orange.

THE PEACE CONFERENCE

After Lincoln's election, William H. Seward (Lincoln's new secretary of state), Republican members of Congress, border-state Union supporters, and representatives of states in the South that had not yet voted to secede attended a peace conference to plan how to avoid war at any cost. The conference began in Washington, DC, on February 4, 1861. For several weeks, delegates from twenty-one states debated ways to keep the Union together by compromising on slavery. Seward wanted to stall for time, keeping these states from making a decision about secession.

Lincoln refused to acknowledge the conference, objecting to its efforts to compromise on the spread of slavery. Eight slaveholding states decided to wait until after Lincoln's inauguration in March before choosing sides. They wanted to see if Lincoln would initiate a war with the South. When war broke out, four slaveholding states seceded, and four remained in the Union.

met in Montgomery, Alabama, to establish a confederacy, or association of states. They adopted the Confederate Constitution to replace the US Constitution on February 8. Jefferson Davis left his position as a US senator and was elected the president of the Confederate States of America, which the South viewed as a new and separate nation on the continent of North America.

The Deep South—the region most dependent on slavery—was gone from the Union. Slave states bordering the North, including Missouri, remained in question. Would these border states also secede?

LINCOLN'S INAUGURATION

In the midst of the crisis, the Lincolns moved to Washington, DC, and began settling into the White House on February 23. Lincoln busied himself with the difficult task of choosing advisers for his cabinet, trying to represent both Republicans and Democrats.

On March 4, Lincoln was sworn in as the sixteenth president of the United States. In his inaugural address, he spoke about the concerns of the South, trying to assure that he would not ban slavery there. He said, "I have no purpose, directly or indirectly, to interfere with the institution of slavery in the States where it exists." Insisting the only way to end slavery was to change the Constitution, he said, "I believe I have no lawful right to do so, and I have no inclination to do so."

Lincoln delivers his first inaugural address from the steps of the Capitol on March 4, 1861.

Lincoln then spoke about his commitment to the country's union, affirming that he would defend it—peacefully, he hoped. He took his oath of office seriously, to execute the nation's laws and to uphold the Constitution. Under the Constitution, states have no right to leave the Union, so the South's secession was illegal. "There needs to be no bloodshed or violence, and there shall be none unless it be forced upon the national authority," he said. He also affirmed his faith in the sensibility of his countrymen and the design of the US Constitution to solve the nation's problems. Lincoln pleaded with the seceded states to think carefully before "entering upon so grave a matter as the destruction of our national fabric, with all its benefits, its memories, and its hopes."

Lincoln ended by speaking of the strong and flexible bond of friendship among Americans, and reminding them that their ancestors had fought together for US independence. He said,

We are not enemies, but friends. We must not be enemies. Though passion may have strained, it must not break our bonds of affection. The mystic chords of memory, stretching from every battle-field and patriot grave, to every living heart and hearthstone, all over this broad land, will yet swell the chorus of the Union, when again touched, as surely they will be, by the better angels of our nature.

The South did not see Lincoln's message as friendly but as a hostile declaration. A little more than one month later, Lincoln was the leader of a country at war.

★ CHAPTER FOUR ★

THE CIVIL WAR BEGINS

Lincoln was president, and the border states were still in the Union—for the moment. They were waiting to see what the new president would do. Would he make an official statement about the states that had seceded? Would he send troops into the South and attack the Confederate forces there?

Hostilities between the Union and the Confederates would soon come to a boiling point. Southern rebels had already taken over two US military forts in South Carolina while President Buchanan was still in office. A third remained in Union hands: Fort Sumter, in Charleston Harbor, South Carolina.

ATTACK ON FORT SUMTER

On Lincoln's first day in the White House, he received a letter from Major Robert A. Anderson, commander of Fort Sumter. The Confederates had surrounded the US Army fort, and it was running out of food and supplies.

As the last Union stronghold in South Carolina, Fort Sumter was a powerful symbol of a united nation. Lincoln did not want to abandon it. He promised that the Union would send provisions by ship so that the soldiers inside could continue to protect the fort. On April 4, 1861, Lincoln sent a message

In April 1861, Confederate troops bombarded Fort Sumter. In response, Lincoln sent Union troops to South Carolina, and the Civil War began.

to South Carolina's governor, Francis Wilkinson Pickens, announcing that the supply fleet was coming. It would be a peaceful mission, said Lincoln.

The Confederates replied by demanding the Union evacuate the fort. Anderson refused, and on April 12, Confederate troops opened fire on Fort Sumter. After thirty-four hours, Fort Sumter surrendered. Within days of the surrender, Lincoln called for seventy-five thousand militiamen from the North to put down the insurrection in the South. The American Civil War had begun.

Lincoln's request for troops set off another wave of secession among slave states. Within the next two months, the border states of Virginia, Arkansas, North Carolina, and Tennessee joined the Confederacy. For the time being, the border states of Maryland, Missouri, and Kentucky remained undecided.

A STATE SPLITS IN TWO

Residents of the Confederate state of Virginia were deeply divided over slavery and secession. Slaveholders resided mostly in eastern Virginia, while many in western Virginia were abolitionists and did not want to secede from the Union. In June 1861, westerners formed a new government and requested to join the Union.

The US Constitution forbids forming a new state out of another state without approval by the state's legislature and the US Congress. Congress passed the bill to admit West Virginia to the Union in late 1862, without the approval of the Virginia state legislature. Lincoln considered the bill for several days before signing it. It was an unusual case, Lincoln stated, made necessary by war. Such a dreaded step should not be repeated during times of peace. On June 20, 1863, West Virginia was admitted as the thirty-fifth state in the Union.

WAR POWERS

As Lincoln waited for militiamen to arrive in Washington, DC, he took emergency measures. The US Constitution is unclear on what powers a president has during a war, and Lincoln had few previous examples to guide him.

His first step was to increase the number of men in the US Army, asking for forty-two thousand military volunteers. He then ordered the nation's manufacturers to operate at full production to make war supplies, and he declared a naval blockade of ports in the South so that no goods could leave or enter them.

After the surrender at Fort Sumter, riots had broken out in Maryland along rail and telegraph lines. Lincoln knew that if

these key infrastructures were harmed, sending supplies and communicating with the nation's capital would be impossible. He also feared that a Confederate spy network was operating in states of the Union.

Under these conditions, Lincoln suspended the writ of habeas corpus everywhere between Philadelphia and Washington, DC, without the consent of the US Congress. Habeas corpus is a legal action that requires officials to prove to a court that they have a legal reason to keep someone in jail. The order ensures that a person is not arrested and jailed without just cause. The chief justice of the Supreme Court declared that only Congress, not the president, has the constitutional power to suspend this right. The president went ahead anyway.

Lincoln faced difficult decisions. He struggled with the reality that soldiers who ran away from the army could be placed on trial and sentenced to death, for instance, while traitors and spies might remain free for lack of proof to arrest them. "Must I shoot a simple-minded soldier boy who deserts, while I must not touch a hair of a wily agitator who induces him to desert?" Lincoln asked. "I think that in such a case, to silence the agitator, and save the boy, is not only constitutional, but, withal, a great mercy."

Edwin M. Stanton served as secretary of war in Lincoln's administration.

Secretary of War Edwin M. Stanton suspended habeas corpus for the entire country in August 1862. With habeas corpus suspended, army commanders could declare martial law, placing an area under the control of the federal military instead of the local police. Anyone suspected of "discouraging volunteer enlistments, or in any way giving aid and comfort to the enemy, or in any other disloyal practice against the United States" could be arrested and tried in a military court.

During the Civil War, the Union army arrested about fifteen thousand civilians under the suspension of habeas corpus. Some were spies and Confederate sympathizers. Others, though, were mistakenly arrested or had simply spoken out against the Union government.

THE FIRST BATTLE OF BULL RUN

The First Battle of Bull Run was the first major battle of the war. It was fought outside Manassas, Virginia, on July 21, 1861. General Irvin McDowell led the Union army's thirty-seven thousand men. Generals P. G. T. Beauregard and Joseph E. Johnston led the Confederate's thirty-two thousand men. As the two armies approached each other on a Sunday afternoon, reporters, politicians, and civilians with picnic baskets watched from a nearby hillside. Most Americans believed the war would be over quickly and viewed the battle as entertainment.

Early reports sent by telegraph to Lincoln were positive. The Union army was gaining ground and sure of a victory. By evening, the telegrams had changed. The Union was in retreat. Wounded soldiers fled along the road, flinging off knapsacks, guns, and canteens as they ran through the throngs of stunned, screaming spectators.

Poor leadership was blamed for the Union's failure. The Confederates, who were less well equipped than the North but

Union and Confederate soldiers fought their first major conflict at the First Battle of Bull Run on July 21, 1861. Confederate troops won the battle.

fiercely determined, won at Manassas. But both sides suffered heavy casualties: almost three thousand Union and two thousand Confederate soldiers died. It was the first of many bloody battles in the war. Lincoln and his cabinet realized it would be a long and costly conflict.

INCOMPETENT GENERALS

Neither side was ready for war, but many factors made the North militarily superior. It was more industrialized than the South, with more factories and better transportation. The North had more people too, with a population of 18.5 million versus the Confederacy's 5.5 million free people and almost 4 million enslaved people. And the North's naval strength was superior to the South's.

LINCOLN'S SONS

In the midst of war, young Willie and Tad Lincoln became ill with high fevers. The fevers were most likely caused by typhoid, which is spread by water contaminated with human feces—a common problem in the days before public sanitation. On February 20, 1862, Willie died. Lincoln said, "I know that he is much better off in heaven, but then we loved him so much. It is hard, hard to have him die!" In their grief, Mary Lincoln secluded herself in her room and Lincoln withdrew from work. Tad recovered, and he and his father became inseparable.

Lincoln's eldest son, Robert, graduated from Harvard University in 1864. He enlisted in the Union army over the protests of his parents. Mary Lincoln feared losing another son. Lincoln did too, and he also feared for his wife's health and sanity if anything happened to Robert. Their son served as a military escort in Virginia, however, miles away from danger.

The First Family (from left): Mary, Willie, Robert, Tad, and Abraham Lincoln

But the North suffered many losses in the first battles of the war. At first, Lincoln was not familiar with military strategy, and he relied heavily on his War Department (the present-day Department of Defense) and his generals. When Fort Sumter fell, the Union army was in disarray, with aging generals in command. Younger generals had to take over, but many were untested and were either slow to act or unskilled in battle.

The first general Lincoln put in charge of the Union army was George McClellan. He had impressive military qualifications, but as the months wore on, he put off taking action, drilling his men but not actually leading them into battle. When his troops did fight, they generally lost.

After more than a year, Lincoln finally replaced the overly cautious McClellan with Ambrose Burnside, who soon led his troops to a punishing defeat at Fredericksburg, Virginia. The month after Burnside's defeat, in January 1863, Lincoln replaced him with Joseph Hooker. Next, in June 1863, Lincoln replaced Hooker with George Meade.

Leading the main Confederate army all the while was General Robert E. Lee. A former Union soldier with family roots in Virginia, he had led the US Marines in capturing John Brown at Harpers Ferry. Lee was a brilliant battlefield commander and an experienced and inspiring leader.

Not until 1864 did Lincoln promote the general who could win the war for the Union: Ulysses S. Grant. He had a questionable reputation; drank a lot; and had been at the bottom of his class at West Point, the nation's top military academy. But Lincoln supported him because, unlike the others before him, "he fights."

THE DRAFT

On March 3, 1863, Congress instituted a draft to fill the ranks of the Union army. Young men had been eager to enlist when the

war first began. Soon it was clear that the hard fighting would drag on for some time, and fewer men volunteered.

The draft required men between the ages of twenty and forty-five to serve in the Union army for three years. As the war dragged on, younger boys and old men joined the army too.

One main complaint about the draft, especially among the poor, was that a person was legally allowed to pay a substitute $300 to fight for him, which few people could afford. Expressing their anger over this injustice, a mob of roughly five hundred people, mostly poor Irish immigrants, terrorized New York City in five days of draft riots in 1863. They attacked African Americans, beating them to death in the streets, and burned down an orphanage. They also looted stores. A regiment of Union soldiers were required to aid the local police before the riots died out.

Riots broke out in New York City over the military draft that Congress instituted in 1863.

ON THE BATTLEFIELDS

Lincoln received regular telegraph reports from the field to follow the progress of the Civil War. In several instances, he visited battlefields to see the troops, check on his generals, and watch battles.

In early April 1863, Lincoln traveled to Falmouth, Virginia. The president reviewed the Union troops there and visited the wounded in hospital tents. Lincoln also rode through the soldiers' campgrounds to visit the men.

After a Union victory at Antietam, Maryland, during which twenty-three thousand soldiers from both sides were killed, wounded, or went missing on September 17, 1862, Lincoln visited the battlefield the next month. He hoped to convince McClellan—who had refused to pursue retreating Confederate troops—to take action and fight. McClellan stalled yet again, and Lincoln fired him in November.

Once Lincoln risked his life to visit a battlefield. On July 11, 1864, Lincoln rode to Fort Stevens, 5 miles (8 kilometers) outside Washington, DC. Lincoln dodged enemy bullets to witness an attack on the fort by Confederate general Jubal Early and his troops.

Lincoln speaks with General George McClellan (right) at the Antietam battlefield in 1862.

★ CHAPTER FIVE ★

AFRICAN AMERICANS, SLAVERY, AND WAR

Throughout his 1860 campaign and in his first inaugural speech, Lincoln had insisted that his main interest was in preserving the Union rather than ending slavery. Yet inevitably slavery became the main issue of the war. Lincoln's stance changed during the war, though, and he felt that ending slavery would be the only way to preserve the Union.

If slavery ended, Lincoln wondered, how could former slaves integrate into white society? If more African Americans moved to the North, how would the North respond? It seemed impossible to emancipate millions of people and set a new course for the country. Lincoln would explore other options first before deciding that emancipation was the only solution.

SLAVE CONTRABAND

African Americans had long known that the war could become a passage to their freedom. In May 1861, as Virginia voted to

secede, three escaped slaves sought asylum at Fort Monroe, a Union fort in Virginia. The fort's commander, General Benjamin Butler, allowed the men to stay. When their owner demanded that they be returned, Butler refused. He stated that the slaves would be kept as contraband, or enemy property taken during war. Word spread and soon thousands of enslaved people fled to the Union fort.

Butler's decision to keep fugitive slaves as contraband of war, thereby emancipating them from slavery, was not something that Lincoln authorized. After speaking with his cabinet, though, Lincoln was persuaded to approve Butler's actions.

In late August, Union general John C. Frémont, head of the Western Department with headquarters in Missouri, went further. He declared that all slaves in Missouri would be seized and freed.

These people enslaved in the Confederate state of Virginia escaped to Union strongholds, where they were considered contraband, or property taken from the enemy.

FUGITIVE SLAVE LAWS

Two US laws, passed in 1793 and 1850, called for the capture and return of fugitive slaves to their owners. The 1793 law allowed judges to decide the fate of any alleged fugitive slave, without a trial by jury. Under this law, captured fugitive slaves could be forced back into slavery in the South. The 1850 law imposed high fines for officials who refused to return fugitive slaves and imprisonment for people who helped slaves escape.

Responding to public outrage, Lincoln signed a bill in 1862 forbidding Union officers from returning slaves to the Confederacy. Two years later, on June 28, 1864, Lincoln repealed the fugitive slave laws.

$200 Reward.

RANAWAY from the subscriber, on the night of Thursday, the 30th of Sepember,

FIVE NEGRO SLAVES,

To-wit : one Negro man, his wife, and three children.

The man is a black negro, full height, very erect, his face a little thin. He is about forty years of age, and calls himself *Washington Reed*, and is known by the name of Washington. He is probably well dressed, possibly takes with him an ivory headed cane, and is of good address. Several of his teeth are gone.

Mary, his wife, is about thirty years of age, a bright mulatto woman, and quite stout and strong.

The oldest of the children is a boy, of the name of FIELDING, twelve years of age, a dark mulatto, with heavy eyelids. He probably wore a new cloth cap.

MATILDA, the second child, is a girl, six years of age, rather a dark mulatto, but a bright and smart looking child.

MALCOLM, the youngest, is a boy, four years old, a lighter mulatto than the last, and about equally as bright. He probably also wore a cloth cap. If examined, he will be found to have a swelling at the navel.

Washington and Mary have lived at or near St. Louis, with the subscriber, for about 15 years.

It is supposed that they are making their way to Chicago, and that a white man accompanies them, that they will travel chiefly at night, and most probably in a covered wagon.

A reward of $150 will be paid for their apprehension, so that I can get them, if taken within one hundred miles of St. Louis, and $200 if taken beyond that, and secured so that I can get them, and other reasonable additional charges, if delivered to the subscriber, or to THOMAS ALLEN, Esq., at St. Louis, Mo. The above negroes, for the last few years, have been in possession of Thomas Allen, Esq., of St. Louis.

WM. RUSSELL.

ST. LOUIS, Oct. 1, 1847.

In an 1847 advertisement, a slave owner offers a reward for the capture of a fugitive slave family.

Lincoln condemned this action. He did not want to anger border states such as Missouri with an act freeing all slaves, even those belonging to slave owners loyal to the Union. Lincoln wrote to a friend, "If the General needs [slaves] he can seize them, and use them; but when the need is past, it is not for him to fix their permanent future condition. That must be settled according to laws made by lawmakers, and not by military proclamations."

AFRICAN AMERICAN SOLDIERS

Although African Americans were free in the North, the military did not allow people of color to enlist. At the outbreak of the war, African Americans such as activist Sojourner Truth requested that the president allow black soldiers to fight against the South. Lincoln was firmly against their involvement, though, fearing that it would further antagonize border states. In addition, many Northern politicians believed the war was strictly a white man's war and felt that involving African Americans would shift the focus of the war to freeing the slaves. Some African American men formed independent regiments to train for battle anyway, and white authorities put a stop to this.

Sojourner Truth helped recruit African American troops for the Union army.

As the war stretched on into its second year, Lincoln began to change his mind. He told Secretary of State William Seward that the forced work of slaves gave a competitive edge to the Confederates. Instead, enslaved African Americans should be encouraged to escape and "come to us and uniting with us they must be made free from rebel authority and rebel masters." As the battles wore on, the death tolls rose, fewer white men volunteered to fight, and the Union became increasingly desperate for soldiers. Allowing African Americans to join the US military would help ensure the preservation of the Union.

On July 17, 1862, Congress passed the Second Confiscation and Militia Act. It stated that all slaves of Confederate supporters who came under Union control would be free. It also allowed African Americans to enlist in the Union army as laborers. After the Emancipation Proclamation, the federal army officially accepted

TURNING THE SHIP AROUND

Former slave and prominent abolitionist Sojourner Truth recruited African American soldiers for the Union army. Her grandson James Caldwell served in the courageous 54th Massachusetts Infantry Regiment.

Truth visited Lincoln in the White House on October 29, 1864. A newspaper article at the time wrote of her, "She had utter faith in Abraham Lincoln. To a friend who was impatient with his slow political movements to end slavery she said, 'Oh, wait, [child]! have patience! It takes a great while to turn about this great ship of State.'"

African American soldiers, and they were formed into all-black units. And in May 1863, the War Department established the Bureau of Colored Troops. Many African American (and white) women also served as nurses and workers, and even as spies.

JOINING THE WAR

As a result of the new law, African Americans rushed to join the Union effort. In total, 179,000 African Americans—escaped slaves and free—joined the Union army, with another 19,000 serving in the navy. At first, the military paid African American soldiers much less than their white counterparts. In 1864 Congress approved equal pay for African American soldiers.

African American soldiers were allowed to join the Union army beginning in July 1862.

The Union army segregated troops by race, with white commanders leading most African American units. One of the first all-black regiments, the 54th Massachusetts Infantry, led by white colonel Robert Gould Shaw, led an assault on Fort Wagner in South Carolina in July 1863. Facing heavy fire, 272 soldiers, almost half of the unit's 600 men, were killed, wounded, or captured. The unit was celebrated for its valor. During the war, 80 African American men became commissioned officers. By the end of the war, the US Army had awarded 16 African American soldiers the Medal of Honor, the highest of all military honors.

Colonel Robert Gould Shaw (by flag with sword) leads the 54th Massachusetts Infantry in a charge against Fort Wagner in July 1863.

COMPENSATED EMANCIPATION AND COLONIZATION

Lincoln worried that even people emancipated from slavery would always be unfairly treated by white society. For political reasons, he hoped to avoid proclaiming a full national emancipation that would free all slaves.

Instead, Lincoln sought other options. In the fall of 1861, he proposed the US government pay slave owners in the border states to free their slaves. This federally funded gradual compensation program could be tested in Delaware, he thought. A model plan would pay $500 for every slave, who would be gradually freed within thirty years. If it worked there, the plan could be expanded to the other border states to help shorten the war. Delaware citizens and the state's legislature were not impressed with the plan, however, and no action was taken. Lincoln would continue to push Congress to support his payment plan.

A second plan that Lincoln supported was for free African American people to volunteer to set up colonies in Africa or in Central America. On June 5, 1862, Lincoln signed a bill to start the colonization project. For the first time in US history, this bill recognized two black governments around the world, including the governments of Liberia, in West Africa, and Haiti, in the Caribbean. He chose to recognize these two nations because they were potential sites for the colonization project. The bill also abolished slavery in Washington, DC, an important first step in emancipation at home.

In August 1862, Lincoln addressed a group of African Americans to promote the colonization project and to urge his listeners to join the effort as colonists. He explained, "Your race are suffering, in my judgment, the greatest wrong inflicted on any people. But even when you cease to be slaves, you are yet far removed from being placed on an equality with the white race.

FAILURE IN HAITI

While Lincoln had hoped to enlist five thousand volunteers, only about two thousand African Americans chose to immigrate to the new colony in Haiti in May 1863. Instead of a better new society, the colonists faced many hardships from the start. The colony's white management was corrupt and had stolen thousands of dollars meant for the colony from the US government. The colonists suffered from starvation, poverty, and disease, and about forty people died. The colony was a disaster. In February 1864, Lincoln sent a ship to Haiti to retrieve the remaining colonists and return them to the United States.

You are cut off from many of the advantages which the other race enjoy. . . . It is better for us both, therefore, to be separated."

That month Lincoln also approved the Chiriqui project, a plan to resettle African Americans in Central America. This project never came together, however, as several countries in the region objected to US colonization there. At home, African American leaders and abolitionists mostly opposed colonization too, pointing out that black people were as American as whites. Many Northern whites did support the idea, but ultimately, US politicians and citizens rejected the gradual compensated emancipation and colonization plans. Lincoln could avoid it no longer: the only option was an emancipation proclamation.

THE EMANCIPATION PROCLAMATION

Lincoln issued the Preliminary Emancipation Proclamation on September 22, 1862. The document declared slaves free—but

only in those states in armed rebellion against the United States. The proclamation also offered Confederate states the option of rejoining the Union by January 1, 1863, when he would issue a final version of the Emancipation Proclamation. If they did rejoin, the Southern states would not be bound by the proclamation. No state took advantage of that option.

Lincoln knew he did not have the constitutional authority to abolish slavery in the United States. But in issuing the proclamation, he pointed out that the Constitution gave him power as commander in chief during war to make laws to take property from the enemy. Lincoln knew that a constitutional amendment would be necessary to abolish slavery in the United States forever. He could do this only after the war ended and with a Union victory.

The Emancipation Proclamation had no legal standing in the four border states that had stayed in the Union. Slaves did not necessarily make this distinction, however. Throughout the United States, enslaved men, women, and children left the plantations where they were held, and with the war taking up so many resources, plantation owners could do little to stop them. To discourage slaves from fleeing the South, the Confederate government issued its own proclamation in December 1862. It stated that African Americans fighting for the Union would be killed if captured by Confederate soldiers.

★ CHAPTER SIX ★

FOREIGN AND DOMESTIC AFFAIRS

While grappling with emancipation of the slaves at home, Lincoln was also developing his understanding of foreign relations. Relations with Great Britain especially became increasingly important as the Civil War dragged on.

BLOCKING BRITAIN

One of Lincoln's most powerful domestic war strategies, the blockade of Southern ports, was tied to international economic relations. Lincoln knew that the Confederate states—which lost their prime agricultural market in the North after the war started—relied more than ever on Europe instead to buy Southern cotton. The Confederate states depended on their ocean ports to import and export goods and receive wartime supplies. The Union blockade of this key source of economic strength eventually brought the South's economy to its knees. It also affected wartime alliances. The cloth-making trade in Great Britain, for instance, relied on US Southern cotton. So the Confederate government felt sure it could draw Great Britain into the war on the Southern side.

Lincoln wanted to make sure European armies sided with the North. At the beginning of his first term, Lincoln admitted, "I don't know anything about diplomacy. I will be very apt to make blunders." So he relied on Secretary of State Seward to manage foreign affairs. He also utilized the skills of Massachusetts senator Charles Sumner, who understood British affairs and who Lincoln appointed as his chief adviser on foreign policy.

Yet Lincoln was not without insight into foreign affairs. He believed that a nation such as the United States had the legal authority to ask foreign allies for help during wartime. Lincoln believed that the Civil War was the illegal action of traitors within the United States. Therefore, it was not a war between two separate nations, and the Confederacy had no right to seek such help.

By late May 1861, Seward believed that Great Britain was close to recognizing the Confederacy as a separate nation. In November 1861, an incident with a British ship threatened to start a war

The Union navy blocks the port of Mobile Bay, Alabama (above). This Confederate port was an important access point to the Gulf of Mexico and Confederate trade with foreign nations.

between the Union and Great Britain. US Navy officer Charles Wilkes intercepted the British mail ship *Trent* on November 8. He arrested two Confederate diplomats on the ship and took them to Boston as war contraband. While the Union was happy at first about their capture, the British were outraged that the Union had violated their neutrality in the war. Great Britain ordered its warships and eight thousand troops to prepare for hostile action in Canada, which was under its rule. On December 9, Great Britain sent an official demand that the two Confederates be released and the Union apologize for its action.

With British ships and troops in Canada, the Union feared the possibility of war with Great Britain if it did not agree to its demands. Lincoln knew the Union could not possibly fight two wars at the same time. Soon Great Britain dropped its demand for an apology but stood firm on its demand for the prisoners to be released.

Lincoln and his cabinet met on Christmas Day, December 25, and decided it was best to release the imprisoned Confederates and to explain that Wilkes had acted without the Union government's consent. The crisis over, Great Britain and the Union returned to good diplomatic terms.

The British government had outlawed slavery throughout its empire in 1833, and public opinion in Great Britain was firmly against slavery. Britain ultimately remained neutral.

IMPROVING THE UNION

While the Civil War dominated Lincoln's presidency, Lincoln also worked to improve the nation. The country's wealth was unevenly distributed, with a wide gap between rich and poor people. Most Americans fell at the lower end of the economic scale. Lincoln hoped to help them raise their status through economic and educational opportunities. He wanted to create stability as well as

to promote the country's unification through federal institutions and national infrastructure. Opening up land for settlement in the West would also improve the economy. With these domestic reforms, Lincoln hoped that all Americans would have equal opportunities to improve their lives, just as he had done.

WARTIME ECONOMICS

The US government spent millions of dollars every year to pay for the Civil War. The Union sought different ways to raise money to pay soldiers; to buy weapons, uniforms, and housing; and to pay for doctors and hospitals for wounded soldiers.

One method the government used to raise money was to simply print more of it. Before the Civil War, individual banks printed their own paper money, and thousands of different kinds of paper money had circulated since the nation's independence. Congress passed the Legal Tender Act of 1862 to allow the US federal government to issue $150 million in paper legal tender, or money. During the war, Congress would approve the printing of $457 million in paper money. The next year, Congress created

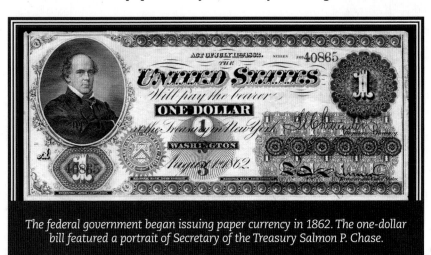

The federal government began issuing paper currency in 1862. The one-dollar bill featured a portrait of Secretary of the Treasury Salmon P. Chase.

COPPERHEADS

Not all members of the US Congress agreed with the economic acts Lincoln signed into law. For example, antiwar Peace Democrats were strongly against them. They wanted peace at any cost, even if it meant living with slavery. The Peace Democrats also opposed the new tariffs and martial law. In congressional meetings, they did all that they could to suppress votes so laws they didn't support wouldn't pass. For example, some hid out in cloakrooms to miss roll calls in session. They attached unacceptable amendments to bills, knowing that important politicians wouldn't vote for them. They also held mass rallies in cities across the North to drum up citizen support. While popular in some states, the Peace Democrats were largely ineffective.

Republicans called the Peace Democrats Copperheads, after a poisonous snake. The antiwar group, however, put a positive spin on the nickname, claiming it referred to the head of Lady Liberty on a copper penny.

a national system of currency, to replace the many different types of paper notes in circulation. The national system was also empowered to lend the government money for the war.

Because the new national bills were printed partly in green ink, they were called greenbacks. The US government did not hold an equivalent amount of gold in reserve to support the value of the greenback, as required at the time. But the US government accepted the money for payment of taxes, and shoppers could use it at stores in the North. The Confederacy also printed its own money, which was worthless after the South lost the war.

The 1862 act also allowed the US government to sell $500 million in bonds. When an individual buys a bond, the government promises to repay that person later on with additional interest. In total, the US government sold $2.6 billion in war bonds.

Lincoln also supported the creation of a national bank to help stabilize the Union's economy. A new law in 1863 created a system of national banks, paid for by federal bonds and overseen by the new Office of the Comptroller of the Currency. These banks were not completely controlled by the federal government, but they were subject to federal inspections.

During the war, Congress passed the country's first income tax to raise more money. The new income tax raised almost $55 million altogether for the Union. Most Northerners saw paying their income tax as a patriotic duty.

OPENING THE WEST

The Civil War dominated Lincoln's presidency, but he also wanted to promote the country's unification through federal institutions and national infrastructure. Lincoln felt that opening up land for settlement in the American West would improve the economy by creating new opportunities to build railroads, homes, and farms.

To promote settlement of the West, to provide people in poverty with the means to own land and run a farm, and to ensure that slavery did not spread into the West, President Lincoln signed into law the Homestead Act of 1862. The act allowed any adult who did not own slaves and who had never fought against the United States, including women and free African Americans, to apply for 160 acres (65 hectares) of public land. The available land was in US territories west of the Mississippi River, and at the end of five years, for a small fee, the US government would grant the land to the homesteader.

Settlers could also purchase it outright after six months of residency and improvements for $1.25 per acre.

The act reflected the president's personal experiences growing up in poverty and working hard to improve his life. In an 1860 speech, Lincoln expressed the opinion that all men should have a chance to own land, saying, "It is best for all to leave each man free to acquire property as fast as he can. Some will get wealthy . . . we do wish to allow the humblest man an equal chance to get rich with everybody else."

The Homestead Act excluded certain Americans, however. The land offered to settlers was already home to a number of American Indian tribes who were not allowed to participate in the Homestead Act.

American Indian nations were angry about being displaced by westward expansion. Some leaders, such as Taoyateduta (Little Crow) of the Dakota (left), fought to reclaim tribal homelands.

US-DAKOTA WAR OF 1862

Settlers flooding west encroached on American Indian lands. In 1851 the US government had signed a treaty with Taoyateduta, also called Little Crow, and other leaders of the Dakota Nation, agreeing to send annual payments and food in exchange for Dakota land. The Civil War drained government funds, however, and the payments stopped coming on time. In August 1862, the lack of money, a failed harvest, and other factors created desperation among the Dakota, who faced winter starvation. A group of Dakota men convinced Taoyateduta to lead a war against the United States to reclaim their land in the Minnesota River valley. Taoyateduta believed that the Dakota would lose but reluctantly agreed.

US forces won the US-Dakota War within six weeks. The death toll numbered about 100 Dakota and 600 US soldiers and civilian settlers. A US military court sentenced 303 Dakota men to death for murdering or attacking civilians. President Lincoln, however, reviewed the convictions to separate Dakota soldiers who had fought in military battles, which is legal in a war, from those who had attacked civilians, which is not. Lincoln reduced the number of convictions to 38.

Due to the war, most of the Dakota in Minnesota, about six thousand people, moved west. A settler shot Taoyateduta to death in 1863. Two Dakota soldiers who had escaped, Sakpedan and Wakanozhanzhan, were captured in Canada in 1865. Before they were hung, a local newspaper reported that a train whistle could be heard in the distance, and Sakpedan said, "As the white man comes in, the Indian goes out."

While some people claimed the land, most poor people could not even afford the costs of moving to the areas, buying supplies and farming equipment, clearing the land, and building homes. This had to be done before any farming profits came in. Of the 500 million acres (200 million hectares) the government offered between 1862 and 1904, settlers claimed only 80 million acres (32 million hectares).

As another part of Lincoln's effort to improve the American standard of living, Congress passed the Morrill Act in 1862. This land grant set aside public lands in each state for the construction of colleges to teach agricultural and mechanical arts, including engineering. That same year, Lincoln also approved the new Department of Agriculture, which worked with the colleges' agriculture departments to develop improved farming practices and new crops for farmers.

THE PACIFIC RAILROAD ACT

To build national infrastructure to link the growing nation, Lincoln signed the Pacific Railroad Act. The act provided money to build a railroad from the Atlantic Ocean in the East to the Pacific Ocean in the West. The railroad would provide rapid transportation for settlers, merchants, and goods. Lincoln would not live to see the completion of the transcontinental railway, but when the system was finished in 1869, a cross-country trip that had taken weeks took only about one week. Towns sprang up at railroad stops along the rail tracks, further contributing to the settlement of the West.

Before the war, congressional members from the South had opposed spending money for infrastructure projects. With the creation of the Confederate States of America, they left Congress, and without resistance from them, many of the acts quickly passed and were signed into law.

Railroad workers construct tracks for the Transcontinental Railroad near Sacramento, California, in the 1860s.

As the end of Lincoln's first term drew near, the difficult tasks of winning the war, ending slavery, and reuniting North and South loomed. Lincoln had much to do.

★ CHAPTER SEVEN ★

LINCOLN'S
LEGACY

By late November 1863, Union armies were gaining victories and forcing Confederate troops to retreat. The Union had gained control of Tennessee and parts of Arkansas, Louisiana, Texas, Florida, and Virginia. It seemed the war's end and a Union victory were in sight. Lincoln began to think ahead, toward reconstruction of the war-torn South and to an end to slavery throughout the land.

PLANS FOR RECONSTRUCTION

On December 8, 1863, Lincoln announced the Proclamation of Amnesty and Reconstruction as part of his annual message to Congress. The amnesty would pardon former Confederate soldiers who took an oath to the United States. In his speech, Lincoln spoke about his commitment to bring the Confederate states back into the Union after the war as smoothly as possible. He spoke in conciliatory terms of finding a fair way forward for all.

Lincoln firmly believed the South should not be punished for leaving the Union. He even hoped that Jefferson Davis, the president of the Confederacy, would sneak out of the country to avoid facing charges of treason. But he also made it clear that he would not allow Confederate politicians to serve in the US government. And he planned to replace Confederate officers of high rank, those who had deserted the US Congress or the Union military to assist the Confederates, and those who had mistreated Union prisoners of war with loyal Unionists. All other Confederates would be pardoned as long as they took a loyalty oath to the Union. Under the

Jefferson Davis, president of the Confederate States of America during the Civil War

plan, a new state government could be elected in any former Confederate state in which 10 percent or more of the adult population had taken the oath. The reconstructed governments also had to follow the Emancipation Proclamation and any other federal laws regarding slavery.

THE THIRTEENTH AMENDMENT

Since it was enacted as a war measure, the Emancipation Proclamation would become invalid when the war ended. A constitutional amendment was needed to abolish slavery, a long-held goal of the president. In April 1864, the US Senate passed the Thirteenth Amendment abolishing slavery, but the US House of Representatives was deeply divided on the issue and did not pass the amendment.

Lincoln chose Andrew Johnson as his running mate for the 1864 election.

Lincoln was running for reelection, and he chose a new running mate, Andrew Johnson, who had represented Tennessee in the Senate before the war. Tennessee had joined the Confederacy, but Johnson remained staunchly loyal to the Union. Choosing Johnson was Lincoln's way of demonstrating fair treatment of Southerners. Lincoln's Democratic opponent was George B. McClellan—one of the generals he had replaced in the war.

After such a long and costly war, Lincoln was unsure that Northerners supported his policies, but he won the November election in a landslide. Lincoln received 212 electoral votes to McClellan's 21.

After his victory, Lincoln turned to persuading congressmen to vote for the Thirteenth Amendment. He let his staunchest opponents know that if they supported him on the amendment, he would give them good federal jobs. Other leading politicians also maneuvered to get the amendment passed. Some even called in bribes and favors. As Representative Thaddeus Stevens noted, "The greatest measure of the nineteenth century was passed by corruption, aided and abetted by the purest man in America."

The amendment finally passed on January 31, 1865. Spectators in the Capitol shouted and cheered. Republican congressmen jumped up and hugged one another. As the news spread across the country, African Americans celebrated, some singing in joy. As soon as the majority of states ratified the amendment, slavery would be forever gone.

In Lincoln's second inaugural speech on March 4, 1865, he stressed his willingness, as president, to accept the Confederate states and their people back into the nation once hostilities ended.

Members of Congress and spectators celebrate the passage of the Thirteenth Amendment on January 31, 1865.

Lincoln gave his second inaugural address on March 4, 1865. He called for the nation to work together to mend rifts that the Civil War had created.

He famously said, "With malice toward none; with charity for all; with firmness in the right, as God gives us to see the right, let us strive on to finish the work we are in; to bind up the nation's wounds; to care for him who shall have borne the battle, and for his widow, and his orphan—to do all which may achieve and cherish a just, and a lasting peace, among ourselves, and with all nations."

THE WAR ENDS

In the spring of 1865, the long war that had torn apart the United States was finally ending. Union armies were driving into the Deep South, destroying cities and farms in their path. Confederate armies were in shambles, its citizens demoralized, and its economy in ruins. Messages from General Grant to Lincoln indicated the end was very near.

General Robert E. Lee had led the Confederate army for four long years, but he finally was forced to accept defeat at the beginning of April 1865. He met with General Grant on the afternoon of April 9, 1865, at Appomattox Court House, Virginia, where the two men signed terms of the Confederate surrender. The Civil War was over.

Confederate general Robert E. Lee (center right) surrenders to Union general Ulysses S. Grant at the Appomattox Court House in Virginia.

CIVIL WAR DEATHS

Four years of war had resulted in a horrifying number of deaths in the Union and Confederate armies. Historians estimate the military deaths to be between 600,000 and 750,000. This was approximately 2.3 percent of the country's population of 31.4 million people.

The American Civil War remains the bloodiest war in US history. In comparison, 405,399 Americans in the military died in World War II (1939–1945). And as of Memorial Day 2015, the ongoing War on Terror that began in 2001 had cost the lives of 6,852 people in the US military.

LINCOLN'S ASSASSINATION

The war had ended and African Americans were free, but many people were unhappy with the outcome. Slaveholders were angered at having lost their unpaid labor force, and many white people in the South felt they had also lost their dignity.

Washington, DC, borders Maryland, a slaveholding state that had stayed in the Union but where popular support for the Confederacy was high. Actor John Wilkes Booth was a Marylander who was enraged by the war's outcome and held the president responsible. Booth learned that the Lincolns were expected to be in the audience of Ford's Theatre in Washington, DC, on the evening of April 14.

Booth was an actor, so no one thought anything was amiss when he entered the theater that night. He made his way to the presidential box, and at a moment in the play when the audience was laughing, Booth pulled out a pistol and shot

Lincoln in the head. Booth leapt to the stage below, shouting out "*Sic semper tyrannis!*" (Thus always to tyrants), the Latin motto of the state of Virginia.

Unconscious but still alive, Lincoln was moved to a small bedroom in a boardinghouse across the street. There, Mary Lincoln, their son Robert, and several government officials attended to him. Lincoln never regained consciousness. He died around seven o'clock the next morning, April 15, 1865. Lincoln's secretary of war, Edwin Stanton, weeping in the crowded room, said, "Now he belongs to the ages."

John Wilkes Booth entered the presidential box at Ford's Theatre and shot Lincoln in the back of the head. Lincoln would die the next morning.

THE SECRET SERVICE

On the same day Lincoln was assassinated, he signed legislation for the creation of a new government agency—the Secret Service. Its original purpose was to protect the federal government from counterfeiters, who make fake money. In 1867 the powers grew to include finding those who commit any type of fraud against the federal government. In 1901 Congress expanded its powers to include protecting the president and the First Family.

In Washington, DC, buildings were draped in black mourning fabric. Lincoln's funeral was held in the White House on April 17. Afterward, a horse-drawn hearse carried his coffin along Pennsylvania Avenue to the US Capitol. There, in the rotunda, Lincoln's body would lie in state in an open coffin as a steady stream of mourners passed by to pay their respects. Two weeks after the murder, soldiers tracked Booth to his hiding spot in a Virginia barn, where they shot and killed him.

Lincoln's body was transported by train to Springfield, Illinois, to be buried. The train stopped in eleven cities so Americans could say a final good-bye to their fallen leader. Lincoln's coffin was accompanied to Illinois by a smaller one: his son Willie would be reburied alongside him. The journey took two weeks, and on May 4, the two coffins were laid in a tomb in Oak Ridge Cemetery.

AFTERMATH

After Lincoln's death, Vice President Andrew Johnson automatically became president, and the difficult work of

President Lincoln with his son Tad in a photo taken by Alexander Gardner on February 5, 1865, in what would be Lincoln's last photo shoot.

reconstructing the nation fell to him. Johnson would not prove up to the task, and historians widely consider him one of the worst presidents of all time.

Nonetheless, as Lincoln had hoped, all the former Confederate states were readmitted to the Union between 1866 and 1870. The Fourteenth Amendment, passed by both houses of Congress in 1868, guaranteed civil rights to all Americans and granted citizenship to people born on US soil, reversing the Dred Scott decision. A clause of the amendment also requires states to provide equal protection under the law to all. This clause became crucial in the fight to end racial segregation in the 1950s and 1960s. The Fifteenth Amendment in 1870 guaranteed all male citizens the right to vote, regardless of "race, color, or previous condition of servitude."

LINCOLN'S WIDOW

After her husband's death, grief-stricken Mary Lincoln and her son Tad lived abroad until 1871. On the voyage home, Tad became ill. Back in Chicago, doctors diagnosed Tad with pleurisy, a painful lung disease. Only eighteen years old, he died on July 15, 1871. Of the Lincolns' four children, only Robert survived. He died at the age of eighty-two in 1926.

Mary Lincoln endured much suffering in her life. She lost three children and a husband, going into extended periods of mourning and at one point attempting suicide. Modern analysis suggests she lived with bipolar disorder and depression, which led to extravagant and unpredictable behaviors that troubled those around her.

In 1875, concerned about his mother's mental stability, Robert Lincoln had her arrested and brought before a judge in Chicago to determine whether she was qualified to be institutionalized. The court ordered Mary Lincoln to a nearby asylum for the mentally ill. A later trial declared Mary Lincoln to be sane, after which she lived in France for four years. She returned to Springfield, Illinois, to live again with her sister and brother-in-law until her death in July 1882 at sixty-three years old.

Mary Lincoln was grief-stricken after her husband's death.

A new era of race relations had begun, and it had an ugly underbelly. Many white people in the South resented the end of their way of life and formed violent racist organizations such as the Ku Klux Klan (KKK). Members of this group intimidated and murdered African Americans and whites who supported racial equality and pushed for racial integration. The Democratic Party, which had supported slavery, won more power in the South. Democratic leaders there passed laws, known as Jim Crow laws, to legally subjugate and segregate African Americans in the South.

In addition, even though slavery had ended as an institution, African Americans in the South labored under a new system known as sharecropping. In this way of farming, sharecroppers worked the land—farming the same land and working for the same owners for whom they had labored as slaves—in exchange for a small share of the crops. Landowners earned most of the profits, however. For this reason, sharecroppers remained in deep poverty, and sharecropping became a new form of slavery. The struggle for equal rights would grow slowly for another hundred years, until the civil rights movement of the 1950s and 1960s, which heralded a new wave of social and legal changes for equality.

LINCOLN'S LEGACY

Among historians and the general public, Abraham Lincoln consistently ranks as one of the best presidents of the United States. His writings and speeches still ring with truth and authority, and politicians still try to emulate his leadership skills. Under his guidance, the country stayed united and slavery was outlawed. Changes in banking, particularly the establishment of a national bank and a national currency, helped fund the nation's growth. The US government granted land for new schools and for settlers, and railroad construction connected people and goods across the nation.

FREDERICK DOUGLASS ON ABRAHAM LINCOLN

On the eleventh anniversary of Lincoln's assassination, Frederick Douglass spoke about Lincoln's place in history from an African American point of view. Douglass was a well-known abolitionist, writer, orator, and social reformer. Born in Maryland, he had escaped slavery as a young man and become a famous champion of freedom. He and Lincoln met at the White House in 1863, and although they did not agree on all issues, they respected each other.

On April 14, 1876, in Washington, DC, Douglass spoke at the dedication of a statue of Lincoln freeing a slave. Douglass spoke bluntly. For African American people, he said, "Abraham Lincoln was not, in the fullest sense of the word, either our man or our model." The president was first and foremost "the white man's President, entirely devoted to the welfare of white men." His first mission had been to keep the country together, even if this meant allowing slavery to continue.

Frederick Douglass

Only secondly did he seek "to free his country from the great crime of slavery."

Douglass continued, "Though Mr. Lincoln shared the prejudices of his white fellow-countrymen against the Negro, it is hardly necessary to say that in his heart of hearts he loathed and hated slavery." In the end, Douglass said, Lincoln was "our friend and liberator . . . and his memory will be precious forever."

This 1943 mural depicts Lincoln meeting with cabinet members and Frederick Douglass (right) at the White House.

Lincoln was a man of his time, with many of his era's prejudices. He was also a man who hated injustice and revered the ideals of the Declaration of Independence and the US Constitution. Justice and liberty are not just for white men, he insisted. They are for everyone. The Civil War tested the strength and flexibility of these ideals, and with Lincoln's trust in the legal process guaranteed by the US Constitution, the ideals survived. Abraham Lincoln left to Americans of future generations the challenge of gradually extending the duties and privileges of democracy to all. As he wrote, "Why should there not be a patient confidence in the ultimate justice of the people? Is there any better, or equal, hope in the world?"

TIMELINE

1809: Abraham Lincoln is born on February 12.

1832: Lincoln runs for his first political office and enlists in the Illinois militia. He serves in the Black Hawk War.

1834: Lincoln is elected to the Illinois State Legislature.

1836: On September 9, Lincoln receives his license to practice law.

1837: Lincoln makes his first official protest against slavery before the Illinois legislature on March 3.

1846: Lincoln is elected to represent Illinois in the US House of Representatives.

1854: The Kansas-Nebraska Act reverses the limits to slavery that the Missouri Compromise of 1820 had set.

1858: The Lincoln-Douglas debates take place from August 21 to October 15 during the campaign for the US Senate seat from Illinois.

1860: Lincoln is elected as the sixteenth US president on November 6.

1861: On April 13, the US Army's Fort Sumter surrenders to the Confederates. The American Civil War begins.

1862: On May 20, Congress passes the Homestead Act, which offers land in the American West to settlers. On July 17, Congress passes the Second Confiscation and Militia Act, which states that all slaves of Confederate supporters who come under Union control are free. The act also allows African Americans to enlist in the Union army. Lincoln issues the Preliminary Emancipation Proclamation on September 22.

1863: The final Emancipation Proclamation is issued on January 1. Lincoln delivers the Gettysburg Address on November 19.

1864: Lincoln is reelected US president on November 8.

1865: General Robert E. Lee surrenders to General Ulysses S. Grant, ending the American Civil War with a victory for the Union on April 9. John Wilkes Booth assassinates Abraham Lincoln during a performance at Ford's Theatre in Washington, DC, on April 14. Lincoln dies, and Andrew Johnson is sworn in as the nation's seventeenth president on April 15.

SOURCE NOTES

7   Abraham Lincoln, "The Gettysburg Address," Library of Congress, accessed November 4, 2015, http://www.loc.gov /exhibits/gettysburg-address/ext/trans-nicolay-inscribed.html.

8   Ibid.

8   Ibid.

8   Edward Everett, "Letter to Abraham Lincoln," Library of Congress, accessed November 6, 2015, http://memory.loc.gov /cgi-bin/query/r?ammem/mal:@field%28DOCID+@ lit%28d2813300%29%29.

8   "The Gettysburg Address: Contemporary Reactions," Cornell University, accessed November 6, 2015, http://rmc.library.cornell .edu/gettysburg/ideas_more/reactions_p3.htm.

9   Lincoln, "The Gettysburg Address."

9   Ibid.

12   Stephen B. Oates, *With Malice toward None* (New York: Harper & Row, 1977), 10.

14   Thomas Keneally, *Abraham Lincoln* (New York: Penguin, 2003), 17.

15   David Herbert Donald, *Lincoln* (New York: Simon and Schuster, 1995), 44.

17   Oates, *With Malice toward None*, 30.

18   Abraham Lincoln, *Collected Works of Abraham Lincoln*, vol.1, ed. Roy P. Basler (New Brunswick, NJ: Rutgers University Press, 1953), 48.

21   Candace Fleming, *The Lincolns: A Scrapbook Look at Abraham and Mary* (New York: Schwartz & Wade, 2008), 32.

23   Keneally, *Abraham Lincoln*, 39.

28   Oates, *With Malice toward None*, 113.

29   Keneally, *Abraham Lincoln*, 60.

30   Fleming, *The Lincolns*, 61.

31 Abraham Lincoln, "House Divided Speech," Abraham Lincoln Online, accessed November 4, 2015, http://www.abrahamlincolnonline.org/lincoln/speeches/house.htm.

32 Stephen Douglas, "The Lincoln-Douglas Debates: Fifth Joint Debate, Galesburg, October 7, 1858; Mr. Douglas's Speech," Claremont McKenna College, accessed November 4, 2015, http://www1.cmc.edu/pages/faculty/JPitney/lincdoug.html.

33 Keneally, *Abraham Lincoln*, 70.

40 Oates, *With Malice toward None*, 184.

41 Ibid., 187–188.

41 Ibid., 195.

44 Abraham Lincoln, "First Inaugural Address of Abraham Lincoln," The Avalon Project, accessed November 4, 2015, http://avalon.law.yale.edu/19th_century/lincoln1.asp.

45 Ibid.

45 Ibid.

45 Ibid.

49 Abraham Lincoln, "Letter to Erastus Corning and Others," Abraham Lincoln Online, accessed November 4, 2015, http://www.abrahamlincolnonline.org/lincoln/speeches/corning.htm.

50 Edwin M. Stanton, "Order Authorizing the Arrest of Persons Discouraging Enlistment," *New York Times*, August 9, 1862, http://www.nytimes.com/1862/08/09/news/order-authorizing-the-arrest-of-persons-discouraging-enlistment.html.

52 Abraham Lincoln, "Upstairs at the White House: Prince of Wales Room," Mr. Lincoln's White House, accessed October 15, 2015, http://www.mrlincolnswhitehouse.org/inside.asp?ID=36&subjectID=3.

53 Fleming, *The Lincolns*, 110.

59   Abraham Lincoln, "Letter to Orville H. Browning (September 22, 1861)," *Lincoln's Writings*, accessed November 4, 2015, http://housedivided.dickinson.edu/sites/lincoln/letter-to-orville-browning-september-22-1861.

60   Oates, *With Malice toward None*, 309.

60   Sojourner Truth, *Narrative of Sojourner Truth; a Bondswoman of Olden Time*, electronic version (2001), Documenting the American South, accessed September 10, 2015, http://docsouth.unc.edu/neh/truth84/truth84.html.

63–64   Abraham Lincoln, "Address on Colonization to a Deputation of Negroes," in *Collected Works of Abraham Lincoln*, vol. 5, ed. Roy P. Basler, accessed September 24, 2015, http://quod.lib.umich.edu/l/lincoln/lincoln5/1:812?rgn=div1;view=fulltext.

67   Kevin Peraino, "Lincoln's Foreign Policy in Today's World," *Wall Street Journal*, February 14, 2014, http://www.wsj.com/articles/SB10001424052702304434104579382990902123538.

72   Abraham Lincoln, *Lincoln on Democracy*, ed. Mario M. Cuomo (Bronx, NY: Fordham University Press, 2004), 176.

73   "U.S.-Dakota War of 1862," Minnesota Historical Society, accessed October 15, 2015, http://www.historicfortsnelling.org/history/us-dakota-war.

78   Donald, *Lincoln*, 554.

80   Abraham Lincoln, "Second Inaugural Address of Abraham Lincoln," The Avalon Project, accessed November 4, 2015, http://avalon.law.yale.edu/19th_century/lincoln2.asp.

83   Keneally, *Lincoln*, 190.

83   Ibid.

85   "15th Amendment to the Constitution," Library of Congress, accessed April 13, 2015, http://loc.gov/rr/program/bib/ourdocs/15thamendment.html.

88 Frederick Douglass, "Oration in Memory of Abraham Lincoln," Teaching American History, accessed September 7, 2015, http:// teachingamericanhistory.org/library/document/oration-in -memory-of-abraham-lincoln.

89 Ibid.

90 Lincoln, "First Inaugural Address."

GLOSSARY

abolish: to end officially

annex: to take control over a place or a thing

Confederacy: the political union formed by states in the South that seceded from the Union. Its full, official name was the Confederate States of America, or CSA.

draft: a system for selecting people for military service

emancipation: granting freedom to a person or group

eulogy: a speech given at a funeral, praising the qualities of the deceased person

Fire-Eaters: radical Democrats in the South who wanted to preserve the institution of slavery by any means

homestead: a piece of land that a citizen could own after living on and working the land for five years

incumbent: a politician who holds an office for which he or she is running for reelection

militia: an army made up of nonprofessional soldiers, often created for a specific purpose such as protecting a community

orator: a speechmaker

popular sovereignty: the right of voters in individual states to decide issues for themselves, independently of the national government. In Lincoln's era, this referred to voters in new territories and states deciding whether to permit slavery.

Reconstruction: the program the US government created and implemented after the Civil War. Troops were sent to former Confederate states to ensure fair treatment of African American citizens and to rebuild the shattered economy and infrastructure of the South.

secede: to withdraw from an organized group or union

sharecropping: renting and working a piece of land from a landowner in return for a share of the crops grown on the land. Many former slaves became sharecroppers after the Civil War.

telegraph: a machine that sends electrical signals over wires. Developed by Samuel Morse, who also invented the Morse code, the telegraph speeded up communication that had taken weeks or months by mail.

SELECTED BIBLIOGRAPHY

Barney, William L. *The Oxford Encyclopedia of the Civil War*. New York: Oxford University Press, 2011.

Brauer, Kinley J. "British Mediation and the American Civil War: A Reconsideration." *Journal of Southern History* 38, no. 1 (February 1972): 49–64.

Ellison, David. "The Civil War Draft in Plover and Stevens Point: A Study in Efforts, Attitudes, Frustrations, and Results." Portage County Historical Society. Accessed April 10, 2015. http://www.pchswi.org/archives/misc /cwdraft.html.

Fleming, Candace. *The Lincolns: A Scrapbook Look at Abraham and Mary*. New York: Schwartz & Wade, 2008.

Goodwin, Doris Kearns. *Team of Rivals: The Political Genius of Abraham Lincoln*. New York: Simon & Schuster, 2005.

Hormats, Robert D. "Abraham Lincoln and the Global Economy." *Harvard Business Review*, August 2003. Accessed November 4, 2015. https://hbr.org /2003/08/abraham-lincoln-and-the-global-economy.

Jones, Howard. *Crucible of Power: A History of American Foreign Relations to 1913*. Lanham, MD: Rowman & Littlefield, 2009.

Keneally, Thomas. *Abraham Lincoln*. New York: Penguin, 2003.

Oates, Stephen B. *With Malice toward None*. New York: Harper & Row, 1977.

FURTHER INFORMATION

Abraham Lincoln Presidential Library Foundation—Under His Hat
http://www.underhishat.org/index.html
Visit this site to learn more about Abraham Lincoln through his personal artifacts and letters.

Anderson, Tanya. *Tillie Pierce: Teen Eyewitness to the Battle of Gettysburg*. Minneapolis: Twenty-First Century Books, 2013. Learn about a real teen's experience of war and how she helped nurse wounded Union and Confederate troops during one of the most famous battles of the Civil War.

Freedman, Russell. *Abraham Lincoln and Frederick Douglass: The Story behind an American Friendship*. Boston: Houghton Mifflin Harcourt, 2012. Discover the bond that formed between two of the most famous men of their era: Frederick Douglass and Abraham Lincoln.

National Geographic—Lincoln's Funeral Train
http://ngm.nationalgeographic.com/2015/04/lincoln-funeral-train
/goodheart-text
Read an article about and see images of Lincoln's funeral train and its procession from Washington, DC, to Lincoln's burial site at Springfield, Illinois.

Sandler, Martin S. *Iron Rails, Iron Men, and the Race to Link the Nation: The Story of the Transcontinental Railroad*. Somerville, MA: Candlewick Press, 2015. Learn about the building of the transcontinental railroad and see archival photographs in this book.

Swanson, James L. *Manhunt: The 12-Day Chase for Lincoln's Killer*. New York: William Morrow, 2006. Learn about Lincoln's assassination and the hunt for John Wilkes Booth.

Thompson, Ben. *Guts and Glory: The American Civil War*. New York: Little, Brown, 2014. Learn about the war's biggest battles and many other interesting moments of the Civil War through vivid stories about the American Civil War.

Vansant, Wayne. *Grant vs. Lee: The Graphic History of the Civil War's Greatest Rivals during the Last Year of the War*. Minneapolis: Zenith, 2013. Learn about Robert E. Lee and Ulysses S. Grant, the American Civil War's two greatest generals, in this graphic history book.

The White House—Abraham Lincoln
https://www.whitehouse.gov/1600/presidents/abrahamlincoln
Find out more about the sixteenth president of the United States at this site.

INDEX

PHOTO ACKNOWLEDGMENTS

The images in this book are used with the permission of: Wikimedia Commons, pp. 1 (handwriting), 2 (handwriting), 26, 34, 79, 83; Library of Congress, pp. 2 (portrait), 9, 10, 13, 14, 16, 19, 20, 22, 25, 28, 33, 40, 44, 47, 49, 51, 52, 55, 57, 58, 59, 61, 62, 67, 75, 77, 78, 80, 85, 86; © iStockphoto.com/ hudiemm (backgrounds); © iStockphoto.com/Nic_Taylor (backgrounds); © iStockphoto.com/Phil Cardamone, p. 3 (bunting); © Independent Picture Service, p. 3 (signature); National Archives, pp. 7, 88; © Internet Archive Book Images/flickr.com, pp. 11, 12; © North Wind Picture Archives/Alamy, p. 15; © Everett Historical/Shutterstock.com, p. 21; © Classic Image/Alamy, p. 29; © Laura Westlund/Independent Picture Service, pp. 30, 42; © Mary Evans Picture Library/Alamy, p. 32; The Granger Collection, New York, p. 37; © Corbis, p. 39; © Bettmann/Corbis, p. 54; National Numismatic Collection, National Museum of American History/ Wikimedia Commons, p. 69; © Bridgeman Images, p. 72; © 'Let Us Have Peace' (oil on canvas), Ferris, Jean Leon Gerome (1863–1930)/Virginia Historical Society, Richmond, Virginia, USA/Bridgeman Images, p. 81; The George F. Landegger Collection of District of Columbia Photographs in Carol M. Highsmith's America, Library of Congress, Prints and Photographs Division, p. 89.

Front cover: Library of Congress (portrait); Wikimedia Commons (handwriting); © Independent Picture Service (signature); © iStockphoto. com/Phil Cardamone, (flag bunting).

Back cover: © iStockphoto.com/hudiemm (sunburst); © iStockphoto.com/ Nic_Taylor (parchment).

ABOUT THE AUTHORS

Catherine M. Andronik is a high school teacher and librarian in Connecticut. She has written children's and young adult biographies about the pharaoh Hatshepsut, King Arthur, L. M. Montgomery, P. T. Barnum, Copernicus, and Stephen Colbert. An avid reader and world traveler, she shares her home with a variety of rescue parrots, and she also enjoys showing her horse in western dressage.

Karen Latchana Kenney is an independent educational writer and editor in Minneapolis, Minnesota. She has written more than one hundred books on all kinds of subjects, from arts and crafts to biographies of famous people. Her award-winning books have received positive reviews from *Booklist*, *Library Media Connection*, and *School Library Journal*. When she's not busy writing, she loves biking and hiking with her husband and young son in the many beautiful parks of the state. Visit her online at http://latchanakenney.wordpress.com.